COPYRIGHT HANDBOOK

for Music Educators and Directors

A Practical, Easy-to-Read Guide

Pam Phillips & Andrew Surmani

Alfred Music
P.O. Box 10003
Van Nuys, CA 91410-0003
alfred.com

ISBN-10: 1-4706-3598-4
ISBN-13: 978-1-4706-3598-5

Table of Contents

Acknowledgements

The authors thank the following people for their input and comments:

Dr. Katherine Ramos Baker, Professor of Music, Choral Music and Music Education, California State University, Northridge, CA

Nancy Bittner, Editor, New York, NY

Katy Bowers, Educator, Kokomo, IN

Becky Bush, Lecturer, Grand Valley State University, Allendale, MI

Mark Cabaniss, President, Jubilate Music Group, Brentwood, TN

Daniel Gregerman, Choral Director/Vocal Jazz Director, Niles North High School, Skokie, IL

Joel Leach, Professor Emeritus of Music and Founder of the Music Industry Studies Program, California State University, Northridge, CA

Denese Odegaard, Director, Fargo Public Schools, Fargo, ND

Dr. G. David Peters, Professor and Head of Graduate Study, Indiana University-Purdue University Indianapolis, Indianapolis, IN

Bob Phillips, Director of String Publications, Alfred Music, Grand Haven, MI

Dr. Lawrence Stoffel, Director of Bands, California State University, Northridge, CA

Karen Farnum Surmani, Early Childhood, Classroom, and Vocal Editor; Music Educator; Lecturer, California State University, Northridge, CA

About the Authors

Pam Phillips

Pam has a broad background in arts management and production, and in the music industry. Pam has been with Alfred Music since 2007 as Managing Editor, Suzuki and String Acquisition. She has worked on the production of instructional DVDs and audio CDs as well as hundreds of orchestra pieces and instructional books. Pam has also been the project coordinator for Alfred Music's revolutionary new method, *Sound Innovations for String Orchestra* and *Sound Innovations for Concert Band*.

Pam's career includes booking and producing concerts for professional artists as well as for school groups. She has administered numerous music camps and planned national and international music tours. Pam has run teacher workshops throughout the United States and has presented clinics at a variety of music conferences. She has also served as an assistant teacher in the elementary string classroom.

The American String Teachers Association (ASTA) chose her as their national conference coordinator for the 2007 convention in Detroit. Pam has been honored several times by the Michigan state legislature for her work with youth music groups.

Andrew Surmani

Andrew is an Assistant Professor of Music Industry Studies and serves as the Academic Lead of the Master of Arts in Music Industry Administration degree program at California State University, Northridge, one of the few graduate-level music business programs in the U.S. Andrew has worked in the music publishing and music products field for more than 30 years, most recently as Alfred Music's Chief Marketing Officer, overseeing global sales, marketing, and product development. Co-author of the best-selling series *Alfred's Essentials of Music Theory*, as well as *Alfred's Music Playing Cards: Classical Composers* and *Alfred's Music Playing Cards: Instruments*, Andrew has also published articles in educational and music industry trade journals, and has conducted workshops on music education and industry topics throughout the world.

Andrew was a founding board member and is a past president of the international Jazz Education Network (JEN). In addition, he serves on the Music Technology Advisory Board at Indiana University-Purdue University Indianapolis (IUPUI), the Technology Institute for Music Educators (TI:ME) Advisory Board, and the College Music Society Editorial Review Board.

Andrew holds a Bachelor of Music degree in Trumpet Performance and a Master of Business Administration degree (M.B.A.) from California State University, Northridge.

A Note from the Authors

We have worked with copyright in various educational and professional situations for over 30 years: Andrew within the music industry, academia, and nonprofits and Pam as a business manager of a fiddle ensemble, an assistant teacher, an editor, and a concert producer.

Our introduction to copyright has been based in real-world experience. This includes the embarrassment of being in error and, in one case, being face to face with a composer who very graciously explained that an infringement had occurred. This has led us to study copyright as it applies specifically to educational and nonprofit situations.

CHAPTER 1

Introduction

What is the purpose of this book?

The purpose of this book is to provide a brief, easy-to-read, introductory guide aimed specifically at basic copyright issues that music educators and directors in the United States face regularly.

Due to the changing nature of technology and the law, updates to this volume will be made at the time of reprints; however, it is always good to verify the latest legal rulings.

> THIS HANDBOOK IS INTENDED AS A STARTING POINT. SINCE WE ARE NOT ATTORNEYS, WE STRONGLY RECOMMEND THAT YOU CONSULT AN INTELLECTUAL PROPERTY ATTORNEY ON ANY QUESTIONS YOU HAVE ABOUT COPYRIGHT LAW.

What are the rights defined by copyright law?

Under Section 106 of the U.S. Copyright Act of 1976, found at copyright.gov, there are various rights associated with copyrighted works controlled by the copyright owner.

These rights involve the following:

1. **Reproduction:** the right to reproduce the copyrighted work in copies or phonorecords [audio/sound recordings]
2. **Derivative Works:** the right to prepare derivative works based upon the copyrighted work

3. **Distribution:** the right to distribute copies or phonorecords of the copyrighted work to the public by sale or other transfer of ownership, or by rental, lease, or lending

4. **Performance:** in the case of literary, musical, dramatic, and choreographic works, pantomimes, and motion pictures, and other audiovisual works, the right to perform the copyrighted work publicly

5. **Display:** in the case of literary, musical, dramatic, and choreographic works, pantomimes, and pictorial, graphic, or sculptural works, including the individual images of a motion picture or other audiovisual work, the right to display the copyrighted work publicly

6. **Performance [Audio/Sound Recordings]:** in the case of sound recordings, the right to perform the copyrighted work publicly by means of a digital audio transmission

How do these rights affect a real-world setting?

A simplified approach to copyright law in everyday use is to understand that any time a work is reproduced in any form, there may be laws that apply. For example, referring to the list above:

1. Right number 1 includes the mechanical right. It is referred to as "mechanical" because audio reproduction was originally done mechanically. Even though it is done digitally today, the term "mechanical" is still used. For example, this impacts creating and duplicating recordings either as a digital album or on a CD. A mechanical license must be obtained and a royalty must be paid in this instance. (Refer to Chapter 5 for additional discussion.)

2. Right number 2 includes the right to make an arrangement of a musical composition. Permission from the copyright holder or owner must be obtained prior to creating an arrangement, and the arrangement will be owned by the copyright owner. (Refer to Chapter 9 for additional discussion.)

3. Rights numbers 1 and 3 include the right to sell printed copies. For example, permission must be obtained to reproduce music and lyrics in printed or digital form by copying, publishing, or scanning. (Refer to Chapter 4 for additional discussion.)

4. Rights numbers 1 and 4 include the synchronization right. This is the right to use music in timed sequence with visual images. In other words, the music and images are linked in synchronization. This part of the law also impacts creating video recordings of concerts. (Refer to Chapter 6 for additional discussion.)

5. Rights numbers 4, 5, and 6 include the performance right. This involves public performances of copyrighted music. (Refer to Chapter 8 for additional discussion.)

How do I find out more?

Copyright law has many gray areas. It is also constantly evolving, particularly as new technologies that provide new tools for reproduction are developed.

This book provides basic answers to questions the authors have received at conferences and in correspondence. The chapters of this book cover each of the above rights and what users must do in order to legally use copyrighted music. A detailed index and a list of additional resources are available at the end of this book. For any questions, consult an intellectual property attorney.

We know that educators, directors, and players want to do what is right. Thank you for caring enough to learn about copyright!

CHAPTER 2

General Information:

What Is the Purpose of

Copyright Law?

Why does copyright law exist?

Copyright law balances the need for the free flow of creative works with the need for authors or creators to be compensated for their creations. Copyright law provides protection for artists, authors, and creators and ensures that it is possible to be paid for an artistic endeavor. It allows artists to have control of their work and to be financially rewarded for their creations.

Compositions, books, websites, and other artistic works of all kinds exist because people expressed their individual creativity and their thought processes to create these works. That is why it is called intellectual property. This is the "work" of creators, including composers, and they all deserve to be paid for their work. Due to the provisions of copyright law, when a music educator or director properly uses a composition, the composer is compensated for the work. Copyright law defines when the use of a work requires permission from the copyright owner, thus resulting in payment to the copyright owner or rightsholder(s).

Why is copyright important to our country?

Copyright is important in our society and for our economy even though it has a long, controversial history.

First of all, copyright is the law.

Secondly, the rights of the creator versus the good of society have been vigorously debated for hundreds of years. This concept was so important to the newly formed United States of America that Congress included it in Article 1, Section 8 of the United States Constitution in 1787.

To quote the Constitution:

> "To promote the Progress of Science and useful Arts, by securing for limited Times to Authors and Inventors, the exclusive Right to their respective Writings and Discoveries."

Other items in Section 8 regarding the powers of Congress include the following:

1. The Power to Lay and Collect Taxes
2. The Guidelines on Borrowing Money and Regulating Commerce
3. The Rules of Naturalization
4. The Establishment of the Post Office
5. The Formation of Armies/Navies and the Ability to Declare War
6. Passing of Laws to Enforce the Constitution

The founders clearly indicated the fundamental value of copyright by including it with these critical components of the Constitution.

There is also a strong argument that compensation for use of intellectual property fosters creativity. Encouraging artistic creativity results in more works, as well as more innovative ideas and solutions. This creates a chain of inventiveness and originality, benefitting the community at large.

How do the laws concerning copyright come into existence, and why do they seem complicated?

The United States Congress passes laws that control copyright. Those laws can be viewed at copyright.gov. Since usages change so quickly, particularly those involving technology, the courts often apply existing law in this evolving landscape. Thus, current laws are applied to similar, but differing usages in the face of changing technology.

Copyright law can be quite complicated and potentially has as many gray areas as tax law does.

This handbook outlines information regarding general guidelines in the United States. Please note that the law changes frequently. Please visit copyright.gov to view any new updates to copyright law.

At the risk of being redundant, it is highly recommended that anything that is unclear be researched further. If legal counsel is required, it is recommended that the educator or director work with an intellectual property or copyright attorney.

A Cautionary Tale

A person we know ended up selling his home to pay the fines incurred when he was taken to court for copyright infringement. He had received legal counsel from his family attorney telling him that what he proposed was legal. The judge acknowledged that he had received bad advice, but that did not alter the consequences. See an intellectual property attorney for questions.

Have copyright laws changed over time?

The law has evolved and continues to do so.

In 1790 Congress passed the first federal Copyright Act. The term of copyright was 14 years from the time of recording the title, with an option to renew the copyright for another 14 years. It did not include musical compositions.[1]

Since that time, United States copyright laws have changed frequently. The Copyright Act of 1831 was the first revision of United States copyright law, and the copyright term was extended to 28 years, with an option to renew the copyright for another 14 years. This was the first time musical compositions were protected by copyright.[2]

In 1909 a new comprehensive copyright law was passed that set the stage for current law. This law set the first term at 28 years from the date of first publication, with the option to renew for an additional 28 years (56 years total).[3]

The next comprehensive law was passed in 1976 and went into effect on January 1, 1978, but between those dates many smaller changes were made. The same has occurred since 1976, particularly as new technologies develop and the scope of the law requires expansion.[4]

Do the laws continue to change?

Copyright laws do not cover every possible scenario that can arise. Interpretation of the laws often falls to the courts that hear copyright infringement lawsuits. The decisions that result then become precedents for future cases. Intellectual property continues to be impacted by technology. Technology is changing so quickly that the courts are frequently called upon to adjudicate cases even if the court has little expertise in creative work.

Are copyright laws different in other countries?

Copyright laws vary from country to country, and each country has the right to change their laws as they see fit. Treaty agreements govern copyright between countries. Treaties can be renegotiated or can expire, changing international laws. For example, this means that a composition may be public domain (see Chapter 3) in one country but not in another. If specific and detailed advice is required, consult an attorney who specializes in intellectual property law in the country in question.

What are the rights that copyright allows creators, and how do they impact educators and directors?

What we call broadly "copyright law" involves several types of rights, as discussed in Chapter 1. To restate briefly, these are rights to reproduce, create derivative works, distribute, perform, display, and perform sound recordings digitally.

Through these various avenues, publishers and composers or authors receive monetary compensation for their compositions. As a generalization, it can be helpful to think of any form of reproduction of a work as something that requires permission from a creator. Because reproduction of copyrighted materials occurs in many ways and takes many different forms, creators' rights are covered by a variety of components of copyright law. The permission to use or to reproduce a work is granted in different ways depending on the use. Each component will be addressed in future chapters.

Here are some of the most common concerns from music educators and directors regarding creators' rights:

1. Using printed music
2. Creating and using audio and video recordings
3. Performing in public
4. Uploading to the Internet
5. Downloading from the Internet
6. Arranging music

What about works I create?

As a music educator or director you will likely create works of your own such as original compositions and lesson plans. You automatically own the copyright to these works providing your employer does not have a clause in your contract that gives them ownership of intellectual property created by employees in the course of their work. (Refer to Chapter 9.)

CHAPTER 3

How to Determine

if a Work Is Protected

by Copyright

Is it necessary for a piece of music to have a copyright notice on it?

Though recommended, it is no longer necessary for music to have a copyright notice on it for it to be protected. Under the U.S. Copyright Act of 1976, which took effect January 1, 1978, music is considered to fall under copyright protection as soon as it is in a fixed tangible form, such as being written down or recorded as a CD or a digital file.[5] A copyright notice generally will appear as the copyright symbol, ©, or the word "copyright," followed by the year and the name of the rightsholder. An example of this would be © 2017 Alfred Music.

What is public domain?

Public domain, often referred to as PD, is the term used to indicate that anyone can use that music in any way, as it belongs to the public. A particular arrangement of a public domain composition, however, could be protected if the arrangement was created in 1923 or later.

In the United States, anything written and published prior to 1923 is generally in the public domain. Works written or published after 1923 are most likely still protected by copyright.

How long does copyright last?

Because copyright law has changed periodically (1831, 1909, 1976, 1992, 1995, 1998), the length of time that a composition will be under copyright protection varies, depending on when the composition was written. The duration of copyright protection for compositions written in the U.S. between the years of 1909 and 1977, inclusive, varies. In 1909 and prior to 1978, various extensions and renewal options were added to the laws; hence, the length of time that a work will be under copyright varies, depending on when it was written and if the rightsholder took advantage of renewal options. The copyrights for some songs have been renewed at various times, and composers have been known to slightly change the music or lyrics of a song in order to maintain copyright.[6]

The copyright status of a composition can also vary by country, depending on the particular copyright laws in effect for that country concerning copyright duration.

Current U.S. copyright law extends protection for the life of the author (or last surviving author) plus 70 years. This is based on the U.S. Copyright Act of 1976 that took effect January 1, 1978.

The time length of protection for compositions owned by a corporation was extended with the Copyright Term Extension Act of 1998. If a composition is a work of corporate authorship, then the copyright extends for 95 years from the publication date, or 120 years from creation—whichever comes first.[7]

It is important to attempt to find the original publication date if an educator or director plans to use a composition.

For additional details concerning the law governing pieces written on or after January 1, 1923, refer to the chart on page 67. A more detailed chart can be found at http://copyright.cornell.edu/resources/publicdomain.cfm.

How do I research the copyright status of a particular work?

To research the copyright for a particular composition:

1. Look for a copyright notice on the printed music or in the CD booklet. The companies listed in the copyright notice can lead you to the rightsholder. If you find a name of a publisher, contact that publisher with any inquiries. Even if that publisher is not the rightsholder, the company may be able to direct you to the correct rightsholder or another source.

2. Review the websites listed in the resources section at the end of this book. Search the online databases of allmusic.com, ASCAP, BMI, SESAC, copyright.gov, the Harry Fox Agency, and the Library of Congress.

3. Check the websites of print music publishers and music retailers to look for copyright notices on the title page of scores.

4. Research the dates of the composer's life and the composition itself for additional information.

A Caution

Many compositions written in the 1930s and 1940s have become part of our culture and are often considered folk tunes, such as "This Land Is Your Land" and "Kookaburra." However, both these songs are still under copyright protection. It is wise to check the copyright details for every composition you use to avoid any possible infringement.

What are common terms that may come up in researching a work?

In researching a composition, there may be references to the composer, the arranger, the publisher, the copyright holder, the recording label, the owner, or the administrator. What do these terms refer to?

Composer: person who authors the musical composition, which could include the melody and harmonies

Lyricist: person who writes the lyrics or words for the music

Arranger: person who sets an existing melody for a particular type of ensemble and with particular harmonies and rhythms

Print Publisher: company that engraves and generally prints the music; may or may not own the copyright

Copyright Holder or Owner: person(s) or company that owns the copyright and controls the rights to use the music; may be the composer, an agency, or a publisher

Recording Label: company that issues the recording(s); however, this party may or may not own the copyright to the master recordings of the compositions or the actual compositions themselves

Administrator: person or company that handles permissions, licensing, and often the distribution of the music

What about music that is out of print?

Music that is out of print is not necessarily in the public domain (PD). Publishers often stop printing a work due to low sales, making the work out of print and unavailable from retailers. Music that is out of print may still be protected by copyright law the same as any other music. Thankfully this situation may become less common with the advent of digital printing.

Publishers no longer have to maintain inventory of low-selling works but can, in essence, print on demand. Additionally, most publishers and many retailers also maintain websites where you can purchase digital music online, 24 hours a day and 7 days a week.

CHAPTER 4

Print Music and Lyrics,

in Printed or Digital Form

Is it legal to copy music in an educational or nonprofit setting?

Generally it is not, though there are circumstances in which it is permissible. Unfortunately, much of the commonly heard "street knowledge" is incorrect.

What determines if copying is permissible?

A few straightforward questions will help to decide if use of print music, including making copies, is allowable.

- Is the use a reproduction?
- Does the use avoid a purchase?
- Is someone denied earnings?

If the answer to all three questions is no, then the use is most likely permissible. If the answer to any of the three questions is yes, then the use is most likely not permissible.

What common uses in an educational setting are allowed without permission?

Educators and directors may:

1. Make a copy of a lost part in an emergency, if it is replaced with a purchased part in due course. Many publishers and music retailers now have websites where you can purchase a single part online. See totalsheetmusic.com, or sheetmusicdirect.com, among others.

2. Make one copy per student of excerpts of works for class study. The excerpt may be up to 10% of a whole musical work as long as that 10% does not constitute a performable unit.[8]

3. Adapt, simplify, or arrange an individual instrument part to suit the ensemble as long it does not change the character of the composition, distort the lyrics, or add lyrics if they were not present before.

The items above are allowed under a provision of the law called Fair Use, as established in Section 107 of the U.S. Copyright Act of 1976, which will be discussed further in this chapter.[9]

What common uses in an educational setting are not allowed?

Educators and directors may not:

1. Copy to avoid purchase. This includes copies made to prevent loss or damage to originals, copies of originals in your library, or copies for rehearsal purposes. If anything you do causes a loss of income to someone, it is not Fair Use.

2. Copy without including a copyright notice.

3. Copy to create anthologies or compilations, including creating binders of copied music specific to a concert.

4. Reproduce materials designed to be consumable, such as workbooks, standardized tests, and answer sheets; print publishers are now releasing many reproducible workbooks, which are a great resource for educators and directors.

For Example

An extreme example of creating a compilation concerns an educator who submitted a string method book to Alfred Music to be considered for publication. The claim was that this was the best method ever. When we reviewed it, we discovered that the educator had cut music out of books published by many different publishers, taped these clippings in a notebook, and asked us to publish it as that educator's own creation. We sent a letter to this educator explaining copyright law!

Is it permissible to scan printed music without permission?

Generally not. Until the last few years, copying printed music meant photocopying. Now there are many ways to copy or reproduce print music. These are still considered reproductions so the following would not be permissible unless prior permission is obtained from the rightsholder.

1. Scanning printed music and posting the files on a school website, secure or unsecure, is not allowed. This is, in essence, another form of copying parts so that the students do not lose them, allowing the school to avoid purchasing replacements.

2. Posting recordings in any form (MP3, .wav, .aau, etc.) is not allowed. This includes both complete recordings or recordings of a part. It is fine to post a link to a legally streamed recording. Refer to Chapter 5 for additional information.

3. Scanning and sending music to educators for all-state auditions or advance practice is a copyright infringement. A license from the publisher should be requested.

4. Scanning for archival purposes is generally not permissible. A school would need to secure a license from the publisher. When in doubt, contact the publisher for a license. As a general rule, if a scan is being made, a fee will be charged. Many K–12 schools have

policies that prohibit scanning copyrighted material into school iPads, Chromebooks, and other tablets.

What about projecting on Smart Boards?

It is permitted to project music on a Smart Board or other projection device one image at a time to viewers who are present where the copy is located. It is not permissible to project the image to multiple classrooms. See Section 109(c) of the U.S. Copyright Act of 1976 for more information.[10]

What about distance learning?

Congress did address distance learning, providing limited usage similar to that of face-to-face teaching. The details of the updates to Section 110(2) and 112 of the U.S. Copyright Act of 1976 can be found in Section 110(2) of the Technology, Education, and Copyright Harmonization "TEACH" Act of 2001.[11]

What is Fair Use?

Educators and directors often hear about Fair Use and think that it means that as long as they are using music for educational or nonprofit purposes, they are free to do anything with the music. That is not true. Fair Use means exceptions for educators and directors that are written into the law to allow for more flexibility in educational and nonprofit settings. The purpose of Fair Use is to balance the public good and the free flow of ideas with the individual rights of the copyright holder.[12] A good rule of thumb is that if anything you do causes the creator to suffer loss of income, it probably is not permissible under the Fair Use defense/exception. The elements of Fair Use include all four of the following requirements under Section 107 of the U.S. Copyright Act of 1976[13]:

1. The purpose and character of the use, including whether such use is of a commercial nature or is for nonprofit educational purposes;
2. The nature of the copyrighted work;
3. The amount and substantiality of the portion used in relation to the copyrighted work as a whole; and
4. The effect of the use upon the potential market for, or value of, the copyrighted work.

The law is not specific and the courts generally have interpreted it based on intent. In determining whether the use made of a work in any particular case is a fair use, these four factors will be considered. Additional details are available at copyright.gov/fair-use/index.html and copyright.gov/fair-use/more-info.html.

As it applies in the music classroom setting, according to the website of the U.S. Copyright Office, the 1961 Report of the Register of Copyrights on the General Revision of the United States Copyright Law cites several examples of activities that courts have regarded as Fair Use:

- Quotation of excerpts in a review or criticism for purposes of illustration or comment.
- Quotation of short passages in a scholarly or technical work, for illustration or clarification of the author's observations.
- Use in a parody of some of the content of the work parodied.
- Summary of an address or article, with brief quotations, in a news report.
- Reproduction by a library of a portion of a work to replace part of a damaged copy.
- Reproduction by a teacher or student of a small part of a work to illustrate a lesson.[14]

Examples of Fair Use

1. The percussionist arrives at the concert and can't find her part. The concert starts in 10 minutes so you copy the part. Later, within a reasonable time, you purchase a replacement part.
2. Up to 10 percent of a score might be copied so that each student can see the score to understand how the parts of a fugue work together.
3. A work in the school library is perfect for your ensemble but is out of print. You are missing two second violin parts and have not found anywhere to purchase them. You may copy those parts.
4. You want to include an E♭ alto saxophone in your full orchestra so you transpose the clarinet part for sax. Or, your band in a small school has no trombones; you might place the trombone solo in the B♭ tenor sax part.

How is it determined whether a particular situation qualifies as Fair Use?

There are no exact guidelines—only the factors listed above. If a situation results in a copyright infringement lawsuit, a court would make the decision.

Consider the following questions:

1. Who would decide if the percentage of a work that could be used was close to 10 percent or went beyond? Would it be duration, number of measures, number of notes, or some other standard?

2. Who would decide if moving the oboe line to the clarinet part because the band did not have an oboe player changed the character of a composition?

3. Who would decide if the circumstances that led to copying a part constituted an emergency?

If an infringement was claimed, either the rightsholder would come forward stating their rights or a court would most likely make the decision.

Understanding the law would allow you to make an informed decision and, if you were ever called to defend your actions, an informed defense.

Educational publishers will do their best within the law to work with educators and directors to determine the appropriate usage and fees for the use of a copyrighted work. If an infringement comes to the attention of a publisher, generally a cease and desist letter is sent to the administration of the institution. That said, lawsuits can and do occur.

How is permission requested for uses of print music that do not fall within Fair Use?

For any duplication not falling within the parameters of Fair Use, contact the publisher through their website for permission. The publisher might not administer all rights, but it is a good place to begin.

Is parody permissible?

Another exemption in the U.S. copyright law relates to creating a parody of a copyrighted work. Be sure to verify, if you are claiming this exemption as a defense to the copyright law, that you are releasing a true parody of a copyrighted work. Note that this exemption only applies in the U.S. and may not apply in other countries.

Is out-of-print music still under copyright?

As was mentioned above, if a work is out of print it does not mean that the work is in the public domain (PD). Publishers often will stop printing a work due to low sales, and thus the music is out of print and not available at retailers. This does not mean that you can copy the music. Copyright law still applies whether or not a work is available for purchase. With the advent of high-quality and fast scanning tools, more and more out-of-print music is being scanned by publishers with plans to sell it digitally.

What do I do when scores are needed for a competition but are out of print?

If you will be performing an out-of-print composition at a festival and require multiple scores for the judges, you will not be able to make copies without written permission from the publisher or rightsholder. Plan ahead, as it might require research to locate the publisher/rightsholder. It also may require some weeks to receive an answer. This is particularly true if it is a busy time of year for requesting permissions, such as when marching bands are planning their shows and requesting permission to use compositions. Contact the publisher/rightsholder to ask if they still have copies they can sell to you or can grant permission for you to photocopy. If the publisher makes the copies, there will normally be a fee to cover costs. Generally you will need to provide the permission to copy to the festival organizers.

Will a licensing request always be granted?

No, but educational publishers work diligently to grant requests when possible. A factor in whether a print publisher or rightsholder can grant you a license is the terms of the contract between the publisher and the writers or copyright holders of the composition—i.e. the owner and/or the administrator. That contract grants the print rights to the print publisher and defines how broad those rights are.

For Example

A pop artist/writer may license the educational print rights of his or her music to Alfred Music. Alfred Music then creates choral, piano, guitar, band, orchestra, marching band, and/or jazz band charts at varying levels of difficulty. That contract may or may not allow for Alfred Music to sublicense that composition for a marching band to have their own arranger create a special arrangement. Even if such a contract grants Alfred Music the right to sublicense such an arrangement, prior approvals may need to be obtained both internally and/or from the licensor for the particular arrangement.

Do institutions of higher education follow the same copyright guidelines for music as elementary and secondary schools?

The principles guiding the use of copyrighted music in an educational setting still apply at the collegiate level.

Are there specific rules or exemptions relating to teaching and performing using copyrighted materials at the college or university level?

There are some unique differences between institutions of higher education and elementary and secondary institutions.

1. The Higher Education Opportunity Act (HEOA) of 2008 mandates that universities or colleges monitor and provide guidelines for the use of copyrighted materials. Most institutions have a copyright policy in place and may have a compliance office with staff able to answer questions about the use of copyrighted materials. It is probably best to start with the staff of the music school.[15]

2. The Association of Research Libraries (ARL) has developed guidelines to Fair Use called the Code of Best Practices in Fair Use for

Academic and Research Libraries. These are not specific to music but are still helpful. A PDF of the code is available on their website.[16]

How does copyright law impact houses of worship?

Houses of worship (churches, synagogues, and others) are subject to the same laws of copyright as other private and public institutions, but with some narrow exceptions. Fair Use rarely applies. The primary special exemption allows for performance during a service at a place of worship or religious assembly.

How can a religious institution simplify the use of copyrighted music via licensing?

Although most religious music leaders try to honor the law and obtain permission first from the copyright owner or rightsholder before making copies, they have found this to be a time-consuming endeavor and an administrative challenge.

There are organizations that make it very easy for houses of worship to abide by copyright laws. Two such organizations are Christian Copyright Licensing International (ccli.com) and OneLicense.net. Such entities work with several religious institutions across North America. They have negotiated agreements with songwriters and publishers from around the world, and the religious institution purchases a license to use that music from the organization. Various types of licenses are available, and the type of license purchased will determine what is covered.

What does this license cover?

Here are the services that such organizations typically offer.

1. **Worship Services:** This covers the copying activities that assist with congregational singing. It can include computer projections

on a big screen, songsheets, bulletin inserts, recordings of a service, and more.

2. **Transposing Music:** This provides transposable chord sheets, lead sheets, and vocal sheets, plus lyrics and audio samples.

3. **Rehearsing Music:** This allows for legal copying and sharing of commercial audio recordings for rehearsal purposes.

4. **Streaming Music:** This allows houses of worship to legally stream or podcast their live-recorded worship music over the Internet.

5. **Video Licensing:** This allows houses of worship to legally show movies for sermons, Sunday school, classes, and special events.

Are there situations that this license might not cover?

Generally this license only applies to assisting the congregation in singing along with the service. It does not give permission to religious institution choirs to copy music for performance during a service.

Does the license vary by use?

License fees depend on the type of license and the organizational structure of religious institutions. These are the different categories of institutions that are typically defined.

1. **Single Ministry:** A church or ministry that meets primarily in one location

2. **Multi-site Ministry:** A church that meets in multiple locations

3. **Event Ministry:** A single event such as a conference or special meeting

4. **Mobile Ministry:** A traveling ministry or individual who uses the license in multiple locations

Why should I follow copyright provisions?

1. It is the law.
2. It is a moral responsibility to be law abiding and to be role models for your students and group members. Today's young people have grown up with the Internet and expect everything to be downloadable for free. It can be a challenge to explain intellectual property to them.
3. It shows respect for your fellow creative artists.
4. It protects you from legal challenges. When an educator or director creates a public profile such as a website or YouTube channel, or has an ensemble that performs in public venues, infringements can become public. Generally a copyright holder would send a "cease and desist" letter to your administrator. This would not be a welcome event for your music program! Again, educational publishers will attempt to be helpful.
5. It speaks to your integrity, especially in adverse financial situations. Many schools and religious institutions are experiencing tight budgets. Some educators and directors have no budget at all for purchasing new music. This is not a valid reason for the misuse of music, however. Other than Fair Use, copying is a form of theft. Most of us would agree that music is our subject matter, but we also teach character building, work ethic, respect for others, respect for rules, and respect for the law.
6. It promotes creativity and encourages new creators of this art that is our profession.

CHAPTER 5

Audio

Is permission required before making an audio recording of a concert?

It depends. The school does not need permission from the copyright holder to record the concert. Once a composition has been recorded and released to the public, anyone else may record it with a proper license, and the rights-holder may not refuse to issue the license. Use of that recording without licensing is restricted. For example, if a school and community group records its own performance and plans to sell CDs or digital downloads, they will need to secure mechanical licenses for all the copyrighted music included on the album, even though permission to record was not required.

Permission from the school or community group will be needed for anyone else, such as parents or community members, to record the concert.

Most professional groups will not allow the recording of their ensembles because they earn a living from selling their professional recordings.

Can the recording of a school concert be kept and played in class?

Yes, it is fine to make a single archival copy of a recording of a student performance of copyrighted music.

Can the recording be posted online?

Yes, but only with a license, if copyrighted music has been included on the recording. Posting an audio recording online is a form of reproduction. The educational music that a school purchases may be performed at your school but not recorded for duplication. A similar rule applies to religious services at houses of worship.

What is a mechanical license?

This is the license that provides permission to place your recording of a copyrighted composition on a CD or digital album. Once a composition has been recorded and distributed to the public, permission to record another performance of it cannot be denied—hence the term compulsory mechanical license. A compulsory mechanical license must be obtained from the publisher or a third-party company such as the Harry Fox Agency. The current statutory rate of payment per copy is 9.1¢ for each composition up to five minutes in duration, or 1.75¢ per minute for compositions over five minutes in duration. In reality, few educational or religious compositions are longer than five minutes.[17]

Can I create my own recording of a composition and post it for study purposes?

Yes, if you secure a mechanical license from the publisher or a company such as the Harry Fox Agency.

May a CD or digital album be created?

Yes, with mechanical licenses. To reproduce the audio recording in any manner such as on a CD, on a flash drive, or online requires a mechanical license for each composition and might involve additional types of licenses.

The key factor to remember is that this applies to any sort of reproduction. This refers only to audio, not video, recordings.

May I sell or give away CDs or MP3s of the recording?

Yes, but only with proper mechanical licensing and payments to the publisher are you permitted to sell or give away recordings of a copyrighted work. It does not matter whether you are giving away the recording or selling it.

Why is it called a mechanical right, royalty, or license?

It is called a mechanical right because in the past recording devices were considered mechanical devices. Thus, it grants the user the right to reproduce and distribute recordings of copyrighted compositions that have been reproduced on CDs, records, tapes, and other digital formats. Granting of a mechanical license cannot be denied. It is called a statutory mechanical license because statutes or laws govern this usage and a set fee exists.

How is a mechanical license obtained?

The good news is that legal duplication of the audio recording of a concert or service is simple. There are three straightforward ways to obtain a mechanical license.

1. Contact the publisher of each composition. Begin this process about 60 or more days in advance of the intended release date for your disc. Most publishers now have online forms, and the process is fairly streamlined. At times there could be some reason that a request takes more time, but that should be rare. If applicable, separate payments will have to be sent to each publisher for each publisher's respective share.

2. Contact the Harry Fox Agency, a company that handles mechanical licensing for a high percentage of music publishers. They have an online form at harryfox.com specifically for short runs (small quantities).

3. Contact a service that will handle the entire process for you. There are many services that handle this. The National Association for Music Education (NAfME) even offers this to its members. Each company handles things a bit differently, but they should verify copyright information, obtain mechanical licenses, process the payments, and possibly even handle duplication of discs and the creation of labels and booklets for you.

What is a cover?

A cover is a new recording or performance of an existing composition. A cover is not a new arrangement and must retain the character of the existing composition. Once a recording of a composition has been made and distributed publicly, it is permissible for another person or ensemble to record it, perform it, or cover it. This cannot be denied as long as a license is obtained. Refer to Chapter 9 for further discussion.

Do the companies that record performances at music conferences obtain licenses?

Most likely. These companies should already be securing the proper mechanical licenses, but it is good to check with them.

Does licensing make it too expensive to produce CDs?

No. Think about how this would work. Suppose you play a concert with 10 copyrighted compositions, all less than five minutes each, perhaps all published by Alfred Music. The mechanical royalties will be 91¢ per disc

(10 compositions x 9.1¢ per composition). Add to that $1 or $2 for duplication and perhaps having some art work done. The school can still sell that disc for $10 or more, leaving a minimum profit of $7, making it quite a nice fundraiser—and everything would be legal! It is also likely that the entire disc could be licensed all at once by the Harry Fox Agency or a service so only one payment would have to be made. The work to set this up may be something that a parent or older student might handle for the class.

May existing audio recordings be duplicated or reproduced without a license?

No. Duplication of an existing recording, whether one released by pop artists or one released by publishers, is copying. Generally, any reproduction of a recording will require licensing. The license required is called a master use license. This must be sought from the rightsholders of the sound recording (usually a record company, an artist, or a publisher), and the license fees could vary widely as they are not statutory licenses.

What licenses apply to existing audio recordings?

There are two rights involved in a single audio recording.
1. The entity that created the recording owns that recording (also known as the master). Thus, a master use license would be secured from that entity in order to duplicate the existing recording. The license fees for this license could vary widely as they are not statutory licenses.
2. A publisher typically owns the underlying composition contained in the existing recording. Thus, you would also need a mechanical license from the rightsholder to duplicate their composition. The rates for this are set by statute.

An Example

You make a recording of a copyrighted composition: "Metroplex," by Robert Sheldon. You own the master of that particular recording but not the composition on the recording. If someone wants to use the recording to post on his or her website, the person would need a master use license from you and a mechanical license from the copyright holder of "Metroplex"—in this case, Alfred Music. If someone wants to use your recording as the soundtrack for a video, he or she would need a master use license from you and a synchronization (sync) license from the owner of the composition. Sync licenses are not statutory and are noncompulsory. See Chapter 6 for additional information.

May existing recordings be posted on a website for students/players to study without a license?

No. Posting a recording of copyrighted music for students is not allowed unless a license is obtained from the master owner and the publisher of the composition. Posting creates a copy, so it qualifies as a reproduction. It is fine to provide a link where students or ensemble members can listen to a legally streamed recording, perhaps to a recording found at the publisher's recording site, or to a legal streaming service.

What is the ℗ symbol that appears on sound recordings?

It is another copyright symbol, used on sound recordings in a tangible form, such as on a CD. If a sound recording is protected by U.S. copyright law, it will have the ℗ symbol, the year of its first publication, and the name of the sound recording's or master's copyright owner. This copyright applies to the recording, not the underlying work.

CHAPTER 6

Video

What type of license is needed for video recording copyrighted music?

A license to create videos with music, whether selling them or not, is called a synchronization license. Music used in audiovisual media (videos, TV, and films) requires a synchronization (or sync) license. The name synchronization derives from the fact that music is used in timed synchronization with visual images. Video recordings of school concerts fall into this category.

How is a synchronization license obtained?

Synchronization rights are exclusively controlled and granted by the music copyright owners or a designated administrator. This could be the creator or a publishing company, a record label, a TV show production company, a movie studio, or a video game company. The owner may have designated an administrator of these rights. Copyright administrators manage the business aspect of a copyright owner's catalog. They issue licenses to use the music and collect the fees from the uses. Tracking down the administrator can require research. Fees are negotiated depending on factors such as importance of the composition, the type of usage in synchronization, and the length of the composition.

What help is available for negotiating synchronization licenses?

For a noncommercial use, investigate the eSynch service on harryfox.com, the website of the Harry Fox Agency, which represents many publishers for video uses in addition to mechanical uses. There are also services that will handle this for you. These can be found by searching online for "copyright licensing services" or something similar.

What are the fees for synchronization?

Fees will range from nothing to quite large amounts based on the factors listed earlier. It may be necessary to pay two fees for the use of music in audiovisual media: a fixing fee for the synchronization right and a synchronization royalty for each copy distributed. Even if you hire a professional videographer to record your group, one of you will need to secure permission from the copyright owner(s) or rightsholder(s) of the musical compositions and master recordings (if applicable) and pay the necessary fee(s).

What if an existing recording is added to a video?

If a pre-existing sound recording is used, the owner of the master recording, which in most cases will be the record label, will need to issue a master use license. A sync license will also need to be secured from the copyright owner of the underlying composition on the recording.

How will anyone know there is a copyright infringement?

There is digital fingerprinting recognition software that searches the web for instances of copyright infringement. YouTube employs such software for music posted on the site. Generally YouTube removes video that might include a copyright infringement.

Can my local cable access channel broadcast our performances?

Yes, provided sync licenses are obtained for each composition.

An Example

A young father we know filmed a beautiful home video of his preschool-age daughters dancing in the living room. He added a well-known country song about a daughter growing up and posted the video on YouTube for the grandparents to see. Within 24 hours, the video's music had been muted. This is one example of how YouTube and copyright holders monitor copyright infringement on the site.

Can I video record our performances for archival purposes, to sell or to give away?

Yes, but with restrictions. It is generally permissible to make a single audiovisual copy of your performance and keep it on file indefinitely. It is permissible to show the video in class. In order to make multiple copies and distribute them for free or for a price, permission will be needed from the copyright owners of each musical work included on the audiovisual medium.

If you do get permission from the copyright owners or rightsholders to make and distribute videos of your performances, you will also need permission and releases from the performers included on the videos, including from the parents of your students or from adult ensemble members. You need to check on the policies of your school district, community group, or religious institution regarding video recording of minors.

Licensing of any copyrighted music that is included on a DVD for sale is a must. In summary, sync licensing is complicated. A music supervisor may be helpful; however, also consider legal help.

How are licenses handled at festivals and conferences?

When an ensemble performs at a festival or conference, often a recording service has been engaged to record the performance. Generally the recording service will handle obtaining the permissions for those recordings and the CDs/DVDs that are sold.

What about videos recorded by parents?

It is very difficult to monitor recordings by audience members. As protection for the educator or director, it can be helpful to include a statement concerning recording in the concert program. A statement such as, "Audio and video recording of this performance is prohibited and is a violation of United States Copyright Law," will likely suffice.[18]

Are videos copyrighted?

Yes. In addition to the synchronization rights granted to use the music in audiovisual media, there are certain rights that are granted to the copyright owners of the audiovisual media just as there are for the copyright owners of music.

Can I show a movie at a concert?

The Motion Picture Licensing Corporation (MPLC) deals with permission to run a movie at a concert and works cooperatively with educators and directors. Since there are many ways educators and directors may want to use a movie to both entertain and to educate their students and group members, the MPLC has come up with a great solution, known as the umbrella license, which covers the motion pictures and audio-visual programs from over 1,000 studios and producers. Under this license, licensees may rent, purchase, or borrow a motion picture in multiple formats.[19]

Can I legally show a copyrighted video in my classroom or religious institution?

This is known as a public performance, and whether you can show it legally depends on the usage. The content of the video must relate to the content of the class or service. As mentioned earlier, there are certain conditions where the educational use will fall under Fair Use, and is thus not subject to a license or copyright royalties. Those specific uses include the following:

1. The performance must be presented by instructors or pupils; and

2. The performance must occur in the course of face-to-face teaching activities; and

3. The performance must take place in a classroom or similar place of instruction in a nonprofit educational institution; and

4. The performance must be of a legally acquired copy of the work.[20]

Take notice of the use of the word "and" after each instance. All four of the above criteria must be met in order for the performance to qualify as Fair Use. If just one of the above conditions is not met, then the use would be an infringement of copyright law. The four components of Fair Use stated on page 24 would still apply. If a video is shown for entertainment purposes only and not for teaching purposes, then it would be considered an infringement of copyright law. An example would be showing a Broadway musical to a physical education class.

Be sure to also see if it says anything anywhere on the packaging or during the introduction of the film that expressly prohibits schools from being able to show the film at their facility. Many films expressly forbid this and indicate that on the packaging or in the film introductory credits.

The main point to remember is that if the video is used for teaching purposes related to a specific teaching situation in a classroom setting then this would likely fall under Fair Use if the above disclaimer condition does not exist.

Examples

Here are some specific examples that are considered Fair Use, as long as it is a legally acquired video used in a nonprofit educational institution.

1. A music educator shows a video on Louis Armstrong in a History of Jazz class. The movie relates to the content of the class.
2. A choral director shows a scene from a Broadway musical in a classroom to students who are preparing to perform the musical at their school.
3. A student group does a presentation to a class regarding the use of music in video advertising.
4. A church choral director shows a video of a performance from a previous church conference to his choir; they will be performing at the conference in the future.
5. A teacher uses a very small portion of a copyrighted movie to teach film scoring.

Here are some specific examples that are not considered Fair Use.

1. Since the lesson plans for the semester have been completed, a music educator shows a commercially produced movie that does not have an educational purpose to students on the last day of class as a reward.
2. A church choir director shows a performance of the Mormon Tabernacle Choir for entertainment purposes at the end-of-season potluck dinner.
3. A music educator presents a movie that does not have an educational purpose for students during a rainy day lunch break.

What qualifies as a legally acquired video?

1. The video was purchased from a legal source.
2. The video was rented from a legal source.

What does not qualify as a legally acquired video?

1. The video was recorded from a TV show or movie broadcast on a cable channel. Refer to the discussion below.
2. The video was copied from a friend's or colleague's copy.

Is it permissible to record television programs to show in class?

There is a big distinction between copies of local broadcast shows and cable channel shows. Local broadcast shows include the major network affiliates such as ABC, CBS, NBC, and Fox, or local channels. Cable channels include ESPN, HBO, Disney, and others. You can make a copy of a show that is broadcasted locally to use in an educational setting as outlined in the Fair Use clauses without getting permission. Cable channels do not fall under Fair Use, and if you use these in an educational setting the use must conform within the educational-use policies of each cable network.

Whether or not you are using a copy of a local broadcast channel or a cable channel, there is still a major restriction on how long you can keep the copy. You may keep the copy and show the video to your class, but only for 45 days, and the video must be shown within the first 10 school days of that 45-day period. The broadcaster is usually not the owner of the show. If you want to keep the copy beyond 45 days you will need permission from the actual copyright owner of the show.

CHAPTER 7

Digital Products

and the Internet

Is it permissible to use material found on websites without a license?

Probably not. Contrary to common wisdom, most content on the Internet, musical or otherwise, is under copyright protection. Most sites include a copyright at the bottom of the home page. This means that even though photos, images, music, sound, and other types of content are posted, they are likely not in the public domain (PD).

What is IMSLP?

The International Music Score Library Project (IMSLP.org), also called the Petrucci Music Library, posts music. While some of the scores on this site are public domain (PD), others are copyrighted, so read the website page carefully. It is preferable to purchase a professionally engraved and researched set of music from a print music publisher to ensure you have a legal copy of the music.

What about inexpensive or free music books that are advertised for download?

If it seems too good to be true, it is probably infringing on copyright. It is not unusual to see websites offering free or low-cost downloadable music PDFs. Often, these sites contain music that was illegally obtained. For example, someone has scanned the book or music and is then reselling it as a low-cost PDF.

May concert videos, PDFs of music, or MP3s of copyrighted music be posted online?

Generally not. This too is still considered illegal duplication and distribution of the content.

Schools and music programs often have their own websites, including secure sites for students. Whether a site is password protected or not does not make a difference. If the site is not a secure site, then obviously the duplication and distribution of the content has greater potential to spread.

Refer to the list of Fair Use questions listed in Chapter 4. The act of posting the file is a reproduction. This means that licensing would be required.

Is it permissible for religious institutions to post music?

It is only permissible to post PDFs or recordings of music when the institution has a license to do so. Refer to Chapter 4.

Is it possible to legally purchase and download music?

Yes. Many publishers and retailers sell music as scores and parts that can be printed or downloaded legally from the Internet.

This has not been as popular as expected for ensemble music, but it is becoming more popular. This may be due to the amount of work necessary to print, collate, and tape together parts. From a publisher's viewpoint, the actual printing is a very small portion of the expense of a composition. Most of the expense lies in engraving, royalties, marketing, and recording. Often, print-on-demand is no less expensive than printed parts.

Is music available for use on tablets?

Many method books are being converted to eBooks in a variety of formats. To do so, publishers need to reformat the method books, adding eBook chapters, indexing, resizing, and correlating audio and video. Though a time-consuming process, this can be very helpful, eliminating the need for teachers and students to carry books around, accommodating the need for paperless instruction, and allowing for on-demand delivery. Ensemble music is also available for viewing on a tablet. Some formats even allow the educator to "write" on the student's music.

CHAPTER 8

Performance Rights

What is a performance right?

Copyright holders have the right of public performance, both to perform a work publicly and to provide permission for others to perform it. The law also provides that a royalty be paid if a copyrighted work is performed publicly.

In the copyright on educational music, it states: "All Rights Reserved including Public Performance." What does this mean?

Many educators and directors have noticed that statement and ask, "Why would I buy music that I can't perform?" The statement is a legal requirement but an exception exists for primary and secondary schools and houses of worship.

Do exemptions exist for educational institutions and houses of worship?

In certain cases educational institutions and houses of worship can perform music without requiring a performance license. These exceptions include the following:

1. Face-to-face instruction at nonprofit institutions by educators, instructors, and directors, including concerts at elementary and secondary schools.

2. Performance of a nondramatic work in the course of services at a house of worship or other religious assembly, as long as there is no charge for the service or the income generated is used for religious purposes.

3. Performances at an elementary or secondary school, including those in the school auditorium, as long as there is no charge for the concert and the performers are not paid.

The exemption allowing performance of educational music also applies when the performance is part of face-to-face instruction, such as during class.[21]

If a school hosts a festival where other schools also perform, is a performance license required?

Events such as this that are held at an elementary or secondary school do not require a license. Often the city will have a license that covers these and many other events; though this should be confirmed, the school does not need a license. If the event is held at a college or university, a license is required, and typically the college or university will have the appropriate licenses.

How is a performance fee for a festival paid by elementary and secondary schools?

If the festival is held at an elementary or secondary school, no license is required. If the event occurs at another venue, typically license fees are paid by the venue to the performing rights organizations, which then pay royalties to the copyright holders, composers, and authors of the music. When copyrighted educational music (elementary and secondary) is performed anywhere other than at the school, a performance license should be obtained by the venue or the presenting organization.

What is a Performing Rights Organization (PRO)?

ASCAP, BMI, SESAC, and Global Music Rights are the performing rights organizations most often used in the U.S. They exist to monitor public performance of music, license venues, collect play lists, collect license fees, and distribute royalties to copyright holders, composers, and authors.

A venue may be a symphony hall, a banquet hall, a radio station, or any other place of business. When music is performed live, the venue will be covered through its blanket license with the PROs so that copyright holders, composers, and authors receive royalties for the use of their music.

How is a performance fee for a festival paid by colleges and universities?

Colleges and universities must have a license and pay license fees for hosting a festival. Fees should already be covered in their blanket license agreements with the performing rights organizations (PROs).

How is a performance fee for a festival or conference paid by a music or state organization?

The organization should obtain a special event music performance license from the performing rights organizations and pay license fees for hosting a festival or conference. In the case of ASCAP, for example, it will be necessary to apply for a license by filling out a form specifically for "Conventions, Expositions, Industrial Shows, Meetings, and Trade Shows." This form will include the details on the event name, date, location, number of paid attendees, number of exhibitors, and whether recorded or live music is performed on any of those days. It may be assumed that since a hotel or convention center may already have blanket licenses with the PROs, these licenses would cover a conference, meeting, or other similar event that is held on their premises. However, those events are specifically excluded from the existing blanket license agreements with those venues. The organization hosting the event, such as the state music organization, should obtain licenses directly from the PROs for hosting their event at a hotel or convention center.

How is a performance fee for a festival paid by a community or religious organization?

The organization must have a special event license from the performing rights organizations and pay license fees for hosting a festival.

An Example

An instance where a performance fee should be paid is when the local youth symphony performs at the professional hall in the city. They may be playing educational music—perhaps a composition by Richard Meyer—but since it is being performed in a public or professional venue, the hall must have a blanket license with and pay a performance royalty to the performing rights organization(s). Meyer will then receive a royalty for the performance directly from the performing rights organization to which he belongs.

How is permission obtained for concerts for which an admission is charged?

When a school or religious institution decides to charge an admission fee for a concert, perhaps as a fundraiser, a performance license can be sought from the publisher of each composition of music being performed on the concert. This would be best done through the websites of each publisher or blanket licenses from the PROs.

Blanket licenses from the PROs are generally not issued to K–12 schools. A special event license can be obtained from each performing rights organization, however. Houses of worship can use services such as ccli.com and onelicense.net to get help with this. It is best to start the licensing process several months in advance of the concert. See Chapter 4 for additional information.

What is a blanket license?

A blanket license is a license from a performing rights organization that covers the performance of copyrighted music controlled by that organization, generally for a certain venue and for a specific period of time.

Is a blanket license required for elementary and secondary schools?

Elementary and secondary schools in the U.S. generally are not required to have a blanket license from the performing rights organizations for copyrighted music performed at these schools.[22]

Is a blanket license required for colleges and universities?

Colleges and universities are required to have a blanket license from all the performing rights organizations to perform copyrighted music live in concert on campus, whether the music is played "live" or by means of recordings.

Is a blanket license required for community groups or religious institutions?

Either the venue where the performances will be taking place or the presenting organization will need a license from the performing rights organizations.

CHAPTER 9

Composing and Arranging

When does copyright begin for a new composition?

As stated in Chapter 3, a new composition is considered protected by copyright as soon as it is "fixed," which means written down or recorded in a fixed and tangible form. It is recommended to add a copyright notice to the composition. The copyright notice generally appears in this format: © Year Publishing Company (or your name). Two examples of this are © 2017 Alfred Music and © 2017 Pam Phillips and Andrew Surmani.

How is a copyright registered?

It is possible to register the copyright of a composition with the U.S. Copyright Office. It is fairly simple, and the fee is reasonable considering the benefits. Visit copyright.gov for more information.

Why is it important to include the copyright notice or to register a composition?

Each additional layer of notice or registration provides the composer with additional evidence of ownership of the intellectual property of the composition. This can become important if a dispute develops regarding the copyright.

If a composition is public domain (PD), is permission necessary before creating a new arrangement?

When creating an arrangement of a public domain composition, permission is not required.

Someone else's arrangement of a public domain composition, however, is protected by copyright; therefore, working from someone else's copyrighted arrangement of a public domain composition does require proper licensing.

May parts of a composition be edited or simplified to suit an ensemble without a license?

Fair Use allows an educator or director to edit or simplify an instrumental composition, providing the revision does not alter the fundamental character of the composition. This does not mean that the entire piece may be simplified. Simplifying an entire piece would generally be considered an arrangement and would require a license. Fair Use is generally limited to smaller portions of a composition, such as a single instrument part. Lyrics may not be altered without proper licensing. See also Chapter 4 on Fair Use.[23]

Examples

What are some instances that would most likely be considered Fair Use?

1. Simplifying the part for a weak cello section of an orchestra
2. Giving parts integral to the performance to a different instrument due to inadequate instrumentation in the ensemble

What are some instances that would most likely not be considered Fair Use?

1. Altering a work for strings to be performed by a concert band
2. Re-harmonizing or changing the rhythm of an existing piano accompaniment to a choral composition

What are the guidelines for editing and arranging?

There are no exact parameters to outline what can be changed without altering the fundamental character of a composition. It is subjective. The intent is to allow for situations in which the music is too difficult for one section of an ensemble, or the ensemble has incomplete instrumentation. Obviously this is a slippery slope with no clear dividing line between "editing and simplifying" and creating a new arrangement. If there ever were an issue, the publisher could seek recourse. When in doubt, ask the publisher.

Are there exceptions for teaching arranging as a unit in a class setting at a secondary school?

Yes. Permission to arrange is not required, as long as the instruction is in a classroom and any performances are only within the classroom setting.[24]

Are there exceptions for teaching an arranging course at a college or university?

Yes. When teaching an arranging course, permission to arrange is not required, as long as the instruction is in a classroom and any performances are only within the classroom setting.[25]

What is a cover?

A cover is a new recording or performance of a copyrighted work. Once a recording of a composition has been made, it is permissible for another person or ensemble to record, perform, or cover it with appropriate licensing. As discussed in Chapter 5, this cannot be denied providing a license has been obtained.

May a cover include different instrumentation from the original?

The instrumentation of the ensemble could be different from that in the original recording. As long as the melody and the fundamental character of the composition are not changed, this is allowed. Again, there is a fine line between what is a cover and what is an arrangement.

What are guidelines for a cover versus an arrangement?

A cover is a performance in which the fundamental character of the composition has not been changed from the original. If the cover is recorded, a mechanical license will be required. An arrangement that reflects any edits or stylistic or interpretive facets of the cover cannot be created or published unless the composition is public domain (PD) or permission is obtained.

What steps does an educator or director take to create an arrangement of the latest hit song or any copyrighted music without infringing on copyright?

1. Learn who can grant permission. Search through the databases of allmusic.com, ASCAP, BMI, SESAC, Global Music Rights, and the Harry Fox Agency to help determine who controls the rights to the song. Understand that the rightsholders listed on those sites may not necessarily be the print rightsholders of the song. The publisher(s) or owner(s) listed will hopefully be able to assist in discovering the appropriate rightsholder to contact for seeking an arrangement license. Alfred Music (alfred.com) and Hal Leonard (halleonard.com) control many of the copyrights, so those two websites can be helpful as well.

2. Obtain permission in advance of creating the arrangement. Most often permission to arrange is controlled by the holder of the print rights, generally a print music publisher like Alfred Music.

3. Contact the rightsholder to request permission. Allow at least six weeks for this process. Complete a permissions or licensing application through the applicable print publisher's website or through a licensing service. The application will ask questions such as intended instrumentation, number of performances, where it will be performed, and if it is intended for sale.

4. Understand that permission to arrange does not include permission to sell unless explicitly stated, so be clear on the application.

5. As previously mentioned, the publisher does not always have the right to give you permission to arrange. See Chapter 4 for additional information.

A Caution

A recent phenomenon we have noted is the appearance of websites that sell marching band arrangements that were created without permission. These sites expect the purchaser to obtain permission to use the composition in a performance. This is a new and most likely illegal process, so be very cautious. Normally the seller would be the one to secure the license from the copyright owner, not the purchaser. Do not assume that because the purchase was made, the publisher will be willing or able to grant permission.

How does the creator (such as a composer, a lyricist, or an arranger) of a composition get paid?

1. A published composer or arranger is paid sales-related royalties, a flat fee, or a salary.

   a. Royalties are a percentage of sales, agreed upon contractually between the writer and the publisher, paid from the publisher's sales. This can include the sale of print music or the sale of a recording. In addition, royalties can be earned from licensing fees discussed below.

   b. Writers are sometimes paid a flat fee for arranging, in lieu of royalties.

   c. Sometimes, but less commonly, a writer is on salary with a publisher to create arrangements for that publisher without any additional compensation.

2. A composer or arranger may be paid royalties for licensing rights when third parties use the music. For example:

   a. Performance royalties are paid directly to writers and publishers based on the reporting of performances and a formula by the performing rights organizations, such as ASCAP, BMI, SESAC, and Global Music Rights.

b. Licensing fees are paid for granting permission to arrange, or for permission to use the composition in a video.

c. Mechanical licensing fees are paid if the composition is recorded.

What if a student or group member composes an original work that we perform? Who owns the copyright to that work?

The copyright of that work would belong to the creator, who would be the student or group member. That person would need to grant permission to others to use or purchase that work, and should be compensated accordingly for its use or sale.

Are there general guidelines concerning submitting compositions to publishers for possible publication?

Each publisher has their own process and will have different needs. Here is a list of commonly found guidelines.

- Choose a publisher that publishes the type of music you write.
- Check the publisher's website to see if and how they accept submissions. Some publishers do not accept unsolicited manuscripts.
- A composer is free to submit compositions to different publishers, and many do. It is accepted industry practice that compositions are submitted to only one publisher at a time. If that composition is rejected, the composer is then free to submit it to another publisher.
- When submitting a book, it is best if at least a portion of it is laid out on paper approximately as envisioned, in order for the publisher to be able to grasp the concept.

- For educational music each publisher has standards for what musical concepts can be included in each grade level of music. Study the catalog of the publisher to be familiar with these things. As a new composer, target the skills in your composition towards a certain age level or ensemble type.
- If a composition is accepted for publication, the copyright generally belongs to the publisher.
- Remember, permission to arrange is required prior to creating an arrangement, unless the work is public domain (PD).

What are some of the considerations for publication that may be specific to educational publishing?

Again, publishers differ, but here are just a few of the factors that may be considered by acquisition editors:

1. Does the composition contain interesting and creative content, including melodies, harmonies, form, texture, and rhythms?

2. Is the skill level consistent throughout the composition? In other words, if a composition is intended for middle school band, are all parts written at that level?

3. Does the part for each instrument contain interesting musical content?

4. Is there a place in their catalog for the composition? Many submissions duplicate one another in terms of the level, style, etc. A publisher's catalog must provide for a wide variety of settings; hence only a few of each style of work can be selected, no matter how good each composition is.

Glossary of Terms

Administrator: A person or company that contracts with a copyright owner to handle permissions, licensing, and often distribution of the music.

Arrangement Right: The right to create derivative works from a composition.

Arrangement License: The license that gives permission to an arranger to make an arrangement of a work and sets the fee or royalty to be paid to the copyright holder.

Arranger: A person who arranges the melody and harmony of a work for a particular ensemble setting.

Audiovisual Media: Media that contains both audio and visual elements such as videos, TV, films, and video games.

Blanket License: The license from a performing rights organization for their catalog that covers the performance of copyrighted music within a certain venue or broadcaster.

©: The symbol that indicates that a work is copyrighted.

Copyright Holder or Owner: A person or company that owns the copyright and thus the rights to use the music. This may be the composer, agency, or publisher.

Copyright Notice: Printed words on the work listing the name of the copyright holder and, generally, the year of the copyright.

Composer: A person who composes the music.

Compulsory Mechanical License: *(See Mechanical License.)*

Cover: A performance or recording of a copyrighted work that was previously made famous by another artist.

Derivative Works Right: The right to create new works, such as arrangements, based on an existing composition.

Fair Use: A defense for copyright infringement for use of works in educational settings providing certain criteria are met.

Intellectual Property: Creations of the mind that incorporate patents, including inventions; copyright, including literary and musical works; and trademarks, including symbols and names.

Intellectual Property Attorney: An attorney who specializes in the field of intellectual property rights.

Lyricist: A person who writes the lyrics for a composition.

Master Use License: The license required to duplicate an existing copyrighted master recording.

Mechanical License: The license required to put an original recording of an existing composition on fixed medium. The maximum royalty to be paid to the copyright holder is set by law. This license is separate from the master use license. This is also referred to as a Compulsory Mechanical License.

Mechanical Right: The right to be able to reproduce music, physically or digitally, via an audio recording.

Out of Print: A piece that is no longer in print but may still be under copyright.

℗: The symbol that indicates that a sound recording is copyrighted.

Parody: A satire of a copyrighted work for the purpose of comedy or ridicule.

Performance License: The license that gives permission to perform a work publicly and sets the royalty to be paid to the copyright holder.

Performance Right: The right to perform a work publicly.

Performing Rights Organizations (PROs): Organizations such as ASCAP, BMI, SESAC, and Global Music Rights that collect performance fees for pieces and distribute royalties directly to publishers and writers.

Print Right: The right to print music and lyrics in physical or digital form.

Public Domain (PD): Intellectual property not protected by copyright, as defined per country.

Print Publisher: The company that engraves and prints music. They may or may not own or administer the copyright.

Public Performance Right: (see *Performance Right*)

Publisher: A person or company that owns or administers the copyright and thus the rights to use the music. This may also be the composer or an agency. The publisher may also be the print publisher.

Recording Label: A company that issues the recordings and usually owns the masters.

Synchronization (Sync) License: The license that gives permission to use music in timed sequence, synchronized with visual images, and that sets the royalty to be paid to the copyright holder.

Synchronization (Sync) Right: The right to use music in timed sequence, synchronized with visual images.

Additional Resources

Websites with Additional Information Concerning the Law and Licensing

arl.org

ascap.com

bmi.com

ccli.com

copyright.gov

copyrighthandbookonline.com

fairuse.stanford.edu

globalmusicrights.com

harryfox.com

icmp-ciem.org

loc.gov/crb

loc.gov/teachers/copyrightmystery

mpa.org

musicforall.org/resources/copyright

nafme.org/my-classroom/copyright

nmpa.org

sesac.com

Chart of Copyright Expirations

copyright.cornell.edu/resources/publicdomain.cfm

Websites for Researching Copyright Ownership

allmusic.com

ASCAP.com/ace (ASCAP)

bmi.com/search (BMI)

copycatlicensing.com

copyright.gov

globalmusicrights.com/search/advanced (Global Music Rights)

harryfox.com (Harry Fox Agency)

sesac.com/Repertory/Terms.aspx (SESAC)

tresonamultimedia.com

Books

Frankel, James. *The Teacher's Guide to Music, Media, and Copyright Law.* New York, NY: Hal Leonard, 2009. Print.

Leach, Joel. *Music Copyright Basics: For Songwriters, Lyricists, Composers, Arrangers, Performers, Producers, Publishers...and Anyone Whose Business or Pleasure Involves Music.* Van Nuys, CA: Alfred Music, 2003. Print.

Monath, Rob. *By the Book: A Simple Copyright Compliance Method for Musicians and Music Professionals.* Chapel Hill, NC: Hinshaw Music, 2006. Print.

Moser, David J., and Cheryl L. Slay. *Music Copyright Law.* Boston, MA: Course Technology, Cengage Learning, 2012. Print.

Winogradsky, Steve. *Music Publishing: The Complete Guide.* Van Nuys, CA: Alfred Music, 2013. Print.

Duration of Copyright[26]

DATE THE WORK IS PUBLISHED	WHEN COPYRIGHT PROTECTION BEGINS	COPYRIGHT TERM
Published or registered before 1923	In the public domain	None
Published or registered 1923–1963	When published with a copyright notice	28 years, plus could be renewed for 47 years, then extended in 1998 for another 20 years for a total extension of 67 years = 95 years total. If not renewed then it is in the public domain.
Published or registered 1964–1977	When published with a copyright notice	28 years, plus automatic extension of 67 years = 95 years total
Created before 1/1/1978 but not published	1/1/1978, effective date of 1976 Copyright Act	Life of the composer + 70 years but not before 12/31/2002
Created before 1/1/1978 but published between then and before 12/31/2002	1/1/1978, effective date of 1976 Copyright Act	Life of the composer + 70 years but not before 12/31/2047
Created on 1/1/1978 or after	When the work is fixed in tangible medium of expression	Life of the composer (or last surviving composer if more than one) plus 70 years. Corporate authorship is the lesser of 95 years or 120 years from creation date.

Index

End Notes

1. http://www.copyright.gov/history/1790act.pdf
2. http://www.copyright.gov/history/dates.pdf
3. http://www.copyright.gov/history/1909act.pdf
4. http://www.copyright.gov/history/dates.pdf
5. Ibid.
6. https://www.copyright.gov/circs/circ15a.pdf
7. Ibid.
8. http://www.copyright.gov/circs/circ21.pdf
9. http://printmusic.org/copyright-info/
10. http://www.copyright.gov/title17/92chap1.html#109
11. http://copyright.gov/docs/regstat031301.html
12. http://www.copyright.gov/fair-use/more-info.html
13. http://www.copyright.gov/title17/92chap1.html#107
14. http://copyright.gov/history/1961_registers_report.pdf (See page 24)
15. http:// www2.ed.gov/policy/highered/leg/hea08/index.html
16. http://www.arl.org/storage/documents/publications/code-of-best-practices-fair-use.pdf
17. https://www.harryfox.com/license_music/what_is_mechanical_license.html
18. http://www.nafme.org/got-permission-to-upload-that-video/
19. http://www.mplc.org/umbrella
20. http://www.mplc.org/
21. http://www.copyright.gov/title17/92chap1.html
22. http://www.nafme.org/my-classroom/copyright/
23. http://www.nafme.org/my-classroom/copyright/copyright-arranging-adapting-transcribing/
24. http://www.copyright.gov/circs/circ21.pdf
25. Ibid.
26. https://www.copyright.gov/title17/92chap3.html